Did

PLYMOUTH

A MISCELLANY

Compiled by Julia Skinner
With particular reference to the work of Martin Dunning

THE FRANCIS FRITH COLLECTION

www.francisfrith.com

Based on a book first published in the United Kingdom in 2006 by The Francis Frith Collection®

This edition published exclusively for Oakridge in 2010 ISBN 978-1-84589-445-0

British Library Cataloguing in Publication Data

Did You Know? Plymouth - A Miscellany
Compiled by Julia Skinner
With particular reference to the work of Martin Dunning

The Francis Frith Collection
Frith's Barn, Teffont,
Salisbury, Wiltshire SP3 5QP
Tel: +44 (0) 1722 716 376
Email: info@francisfrith.co.uk
www.francisfrith.com

Printed and bound in Malaysia

Front Cover: **PLYMOUTH, ONION SELLERS 1907** 59208p

The colour-tinting is for illustrative purposes only, and is not intended to be historically accurate

CONTENTS

INTRODUCTION

The bustling modern city of Plymouth that we see today is not the city that residents and visitors alike would have known before the Second World War. The naval bases and dockyards of Devonport made the area a prime target for the Luftwaffe. Even by the standards of the worst wartime blitzes Plymouth suffered badly, being devastated beyond recognition. The heart of the old city was torn out, mostly during a big raid during one terrible night in March 1941, the most intense suffered by any British city in the war. 10,000 old buildings were destroyed, and 70,000 more were damaged by high explosive and firestorm. By the end of the war, 1,172 civilians had died as a result of the air raids. All we have to remember the old Plymouth by is archive film, photographs such as those in this book, and memories of survivors.

Plymouth rose again from the ashes of conflict, although few who remembered the old city were happy with the new. However, not all of the old Plymouth was lost. Tourists still make a first stop at Plymouth Hoe to see the spot where Sir Francis Drake may or may not have played a famous game of bowls as the Spanish Armada was spotted, waiting for the wind and tide to turn in his favour. A stroll through the Barbican to Sutton Harbour, which the bombs mostly spared, gives a feel of the old Plymouth that the Elizabethan sea-dogs Drake, Frobisher, Hawkins and Raleigh might have known. Some old city landmarks still remain: locals meet at Derry's Cross as they always did, and sailors continue to throng Union Street on Saturday nights.

Plymouth is now a major ferry port, with daily sailings to Roscoff in Brittany and regular crossings to Santander in northern Spain. The Navy are always active in Plymouth Sound, making the city a ship-spotters paradise.

Stand on the Promenade on a clear day and turn through 360 degrees, and all around are reminders of Plymouth's past. To the north are the blue hills of Dartmoor, source of the tin that caused the port to come into existence. West is the entrance to the Tamar, home to the frigates, aircraft carriers and submarines which slip in and out of port in all weathers, even in peacetime. Merchantmen anchor in the lee of the Breakwater, ready to discharge their cargoes of petrol and fertiliser on the wharves of the Plym, and trawlers set sail from a largely unchanged Barbican for the fishing grounds. And on the horizon, the Eddystone light winks unceasingly, a beacon for mariners heading for one of Britain's great ports.

BEDFORD STREET 1913 65976

DEVON DIALECT WORDS AND PHRASES

'Janners' - people born in Plymouth, a less formal term than Plymothians. A 'janner' originally described a person who lived within sight of the sea, but is now used more generally for inhabitants of the whole city.

'Guz' - a Royal Navy term for Devonport.

'Bloin' a (h)ooley' - very windy.

'You gert lummock' - you great fool.

'Mitching' - playing truant.

'Smeeching' - smoking, as with a fire, so a **'smeech mark'** is a sooty mark or a smudge.

'Right maid?' and **'Right boy?'** - a standard greeting to men and women of any age.

'Over the way' - over there.

'Dimpsy' - twilight.

'Ow be you?' - how are you?

'Teddies' - taties, spuds, potatoes.

'Shop fuddling' - window shopping.

'You be maiz you be!' - you're mad!

HAUNTED PLYMOUTH

The ABC cinema, which was built on the site of the old Theatre Royal, is supposed to be haunted by a number of ghosts. In December 2005 a paranormal investigation was carried out by 'Magic2k', which claimed that the hauntings were carried out by a lady called either Winnie or Minnie, a man called Jack and a small girl called Jessica. In Screen 2, Jessica was supposed to be responsible for affecting the lights, banging noises and touching the investigators during a seance.

Since the Second World War, the Master Ropemaker's House at Plymouth's Naval Dockyard has become known as one of Plymouth's most haunted houses. One of the reported sightings has been that of a young girl in Victorian dress seen playing in the house, and the ghost of a bearded sailor is also said to haunt the building. The nearby Hangman's Cell in the Dockyard, which contains what is believed to be the only remaining working gallows in Britain and was reportedly the scene of numerous executions during the Napoleonic Wars, is also said to be an area of significant ghostly activity.

Greenbank Hospital, originally known as the Prince of Wales Hospital, was supposed to be haunted by a ghost known as Lady Albertha, who used to appear beside the cots of sick children. Her appearance meant that the children were sure to recover, no matter how sick they were. The hospital has now closed and the site has been redeveloped.

Across the water at Mount Edgcumbe, the building known as 'Lady Emma's Cottage' (now a private residence) was once said to be haunted by the ghost of an unfortunate lady: she was murdered by a thief who also chopped off one of her hands to steal her rings.

PLYMOUTH MISCELLANY

Plymouth grew from several small settlements, one of the earliest being Mountbatten, at the mouth of the Plym. The site of an Iron Age cemetery, it is thought to have been a trading post from as early as 1,000BC, and in Roman times exported cattle, hides and tin. Opposite Mountbatten, the small fishing village of Sutton grew around the sheltered harbour of Sutton Pool; it eventually became a town when it was granted a market by Henry III. By this time, ships loading tin from the rich port of Plympton had started to use Sutton too, and a lively trade was developing. Fish, hides, lead, wool and cloth were exported, while iron, fruit, wine, onions and garlic were landed.

Plymouth struggled economically for the first half of the 18th century. Although there was a thriving fishing trade, particularly for pilchards, Plymouth has never figured near the top of the table as a commercial port because of its isolation and the lack of nearby markets. Bristol and Liverpool made fortunes from the slave trade, and London's demands for commodities ensured that her ports were always busy, but Plymouth had to rely on war to provide the catalyst for change: from 1756 a succession of conflicts - the Seven Years' War, the American War of Independence, and the Napoleonic Wars - caused an upturn in Plymouth's fortunes.

Plymouth's historical isolation was eased in 1758 with the completion of the Great West Road, but it still took twelve hours to reach Exeter!

SMEATON'S TOWER 1890 22365

THE VIEW FROM THE PIER 1892 30590

During the Civil War, the strongly Puritan Plymouth took the side of
Parliament against Charles I. Plymouth was isolated, as Barnstaple,
Bideford and Exeter were all captured by the Royalists, and Royalist
ships blockaded the Sound. The 9,000 Parliamentarian troops
garrisoned at Plymouth held out under siege for two years, winning
a famous victory in December 1643 in the battle which raged around
Tothill and Freedom Park. Plymouth was eventually relieved in March
1645 by forces of Cromwell and Fairfax.

After the Civil War and the restoration of the monarchy,
Charles II decided that Plymouth's defences needed
strengthening, and commissioned the building of the Citadel.
One of the finest and largest restoration forts in the country, it
boasted upon completion 152 guns, some of which faced the
city as a reminder to Plymothians not to side against the king
again. The Citadel can be seen in photograph 30590, above. It
is now home to 29 Commando Regiment Royal Artillery.

For many years the Mount Batten peninsula was an RAF flying boat base, from where Sunderland flying boats hunted down German U-boats during the Second World War. The huge hangers in which these flying boats were stored can still be seen.

The Barbican sits alongside the ancient fishing quay of Sutton Pool, the original port of Plymouth (see photograph 22474, below). From here, Elizabethan sailors, merchants and privateers set sail in search of profit and adventure on the high seas. The city's fish market was located here until the late 1990s, when it moved across the harbour to a new purpose-built dock.

THE BARBICAN 1890 22474

Before the construction of the Tamar suspension bridge in 1961, the ferry at Torpoint was one of the few ways to cross the river. Ferries had crossed at this point since the 18th century, carrying not only people, carriages and goods but, from 1800, the post for the Truro coach. 'Jemima', built at Stonehouse, became the first steam ferry in service in 1826, but was quickly replaced by steam driven chain ferries. The ferry still makes regular journeys across the Tamar, taking workers across to Devonport Dockyard and the city of Plymouth.

DEVONPORT, TORPOINT FERRY BRIDGE 1890 22462

THE GUILDHALL AND THE POST OFFICE 1889 22388

Plymouth's impressive Guildhall (see photograph 22388, above) was built in 1874, a masterpiece of elaborate Victorian Gothic. During the Second World War it was reduced to a mere shell, but it has since been restored to its original glory. Its tower is a noted landmark over the city.

The city of Plymouth has given its name to some 40 other Plymouths around the English-speaking world. The Pilgrim Fathers put in to Plymouth for repairs and provisions in 1620 before sailing to the New World, the final point of departure from mainland Britain of the 'Mayflower', eventually to land near that part of America still known as Plymouth Rock.

The South African Monument in Plymouth commemorates Queen Victoria's grandson, Christian Victor, Prince of Schleswig Holstein, who died in the Boer War. It also serves as a memorial to the men of the Gloucestershire, Somerset and Devonshire Regiments who died in the same campaign.

George Street was once the very heart of the old city, but was almost entirely destroyed in the blitz of the Second World War. Today, a short section behind the Theatre Royal is all that is left. Photograph 30597, below, shows Derry's Clock Tower, which was given to the city in 1862 by William Derry during his second mayoralty, to commemorate the marriage of the Prince of Wales (later Edward VII) to the Danish Princess Alexandra; it was known as the 'four-faced deceiver', because all four clocks told different times. The clock still stands behind the new Theatre Royal. The photograph also shows the offices of the Great Western Railway in the background, left-hand side.

GEORGE STREET 1892 30597

The year 1295 saw an event that was to point the way for future developments when Edward I assembled the fleet at Plymouth for the first time. The port occupies a crucial strategic position guarding the Western Approaches; it was this factor that was to cement Plymouth's importance, and was probably a consideration when Henry VI granted the borough charter in 1439.

The Palladian splendour of Mutley Baptist Chapel dates from 1868 (photograph 22421, right). George Street Baptist, near St Andrew's, was bursting at the seams and so a new daughter church was built at Mutley. By 1876 it had broken away from George Street and become a congregation in its own right. The first pastor at Mutley was Rev Benwell Bird, who held the post for 23 years and was very popular, not only with his own flock but with all denominations. Mutley Baptist was undamaged during the Second World War, whereas George Street Baptist was destroyed in 1941, and a new chapel was built on Catherine Street.

A sign of the port's growing stature was the building in 1698 of Winstanley's 120ft lighthouse on the Eddystone Rocks fourteen miles south of the Hoe, the first in a series of four that would culminate in the current lighthouse, built by Douglas in 1882. Photograph 22365 (page 7) shows the third lighthouse, which went into action in 1759, built in masonry by John Smeaton (the previous two had been wooden). Smeaton dovetailed blocks of Portland stone to produce a structure which could withstand the worst storms, and which revolutionised lighthouse design; its light shone for 120 years. Smeaton's lighthouse was replaced by the present Eddystone lighthouse in 1882, because its foundations were being eroded. The top section was brought back to Plymouth and reassembled on the Hoe.

MUTLEY BAPTIST CHAPEL 1890 22421

THE BARBICAN AND THE FISH MARKET 1904 52405

Photograph 52405, above, of fishing boats at the Barbican illustrates the changeover from sail to steam.; only eight years before this photograph was taken, the Barbican had seen its first steam trawler, the 'Reginald', tying up alongside the newly-opened fish market. At that time the 'Reginald' would have been vying for catches with the fifty or so sail trawlers, each of 30-40 tons, that worked from here. The fish market was built on an extension to John Hawkins's original quay, built in 1573, and the line dividing the extension from the original can still be seen in the cobbles today.

Near the brow of North Hill was Plymouth's first hospital, founded by the Franciscans in 1300, originally as a leper house.

Photograph 65981 (below) shows a number of paddle steamers around Plymouth's pier - piers were originally intended to be jetties leading to a landing stage for such boats, but they soon became fashionable promenades extending over the sea. The paddle steamers at Plymouth ran trips to the River Yealm and as far west as Looe. In a curious echo of history, many of today's tourist boats leave from the site of the old pier for similar destinations, and also for cruises up the Tamar. Modern excursion boats are diesel rather than steam, and have propellers instead of paddle wheels. Paddlers lasted longer than is generally known, however: the dockyard was using paddle tugs until the mid 1980s.

PADDLE STEAMERS AT THE PIER 1913 65981

THE HOE, SMEATON'S TOWER AND THE BANDSTAND 1913 65980

The stone pavilion seen on the left of this photograph, and known to Plymothians as the 'Wedding Cake', was built in 1891-92 when Alderman Harris was mayor. The garden directly below it is now a garden of remembrance to the dead of Dunkirk, Normandy, Korea, Malaysia and other campaigns.

ST ANDREW'S CROSS 1895 36320

MATTHEWS'S
CONFECTIONERY
AND
RESTAURANT
ESTABLISHED
MACHINE
BREAD BAKERY
67 HIGH S
MANUFACTORY
FOR JAM & S
HIGH

Photograph 36320, opposite, shows a lost view of Plymouth. St Andrew's Cross was destroyed in the blitz of the Second World War, and all that remains is the copper cross from the top, now displayed in the north aisle of the rebuilt St Andrew's Church.

Devonport stands to the west of the city of Plymouth, and is the newest of the three towns that make up Devon's largest urban area. In Lord Nelson's day the town was known simply as 'Dock' or 'Plymouth Dock', only acquiring its present name in 1824. It is probable that Devonport abandoned its earlier name as a gesture of independence. A huge community, both military and trading, grew around the naval yards, with thousands of homes to cater for dockworkers and public houses in which to entertain shore-bound sailors.

Several memorable voyages of exploration and discovery began from Plymouth; for example, Captain Cook left from Plymouth in 1768 on his voyage to chart New Zealand, and Charles Darwin sailed from here aboard the 'Beagle' in 1831. The observations that Darwin made on his voyage inspired his revolutionary theory about evolution, published as 'The Origin of Species', which questioned the account of the creation of the world in the Bible. A plaque on the Barbican also commemorates the departure from Plymouth in May 1839 of the 'Tory', the pioneer ship in the colonisation of New Zealand.

The Elizabethan House on New Street offers a fascinating glimpse into Plymouth's past. This timber-framed house in the Barbican area was a Tudor sea-captain's home. It jetties out over a narrow, cobbled street, and has its original windows, ceiling beams and a spiral staircase winding around an old ship's mast. The beautifully restored rooms on three floors are furnished with period furniture and fabrics.

The building of Plymouth's Roman Catholic Cathedral of St Mary and St Boniface was started by Bishop Vaughan in 1858, and the cathedral was consecrated in 1860. The architects were Joseph and Charles Hansom (Joseph also designed the Hansom Cab). The 207ft-high spire was added in 1867. The Lady Chapel was restored in 1921; photograph 22412 (opposite) shows, in addition to Mary, four other stone figures: King David, the Saints Joachim and Anne, and John the Baptist.

In the early 19th century, sailors discharged at Plymouth after the end of the Napoleonic Wars were often signed up by smuggling gangs and put to work on the many boats running illegal goods through Cawsand Bay, which was the headquarters of Devon smuggling. Smuggling has been romanticised in folklore, fiction and film, but was actually a vicious and violent trade, full of intimidation and corruption in high places. Nevertheless, customs duties at this time were very much resented, and smuggling was a way of life for large numbers of people in the West Country. At the beginning of the 19th century it has been estimated that each year more brandy and rum was probably smuggled into England through Devon, Dorset and Cornwall than was imported legally into London.

DEVONPORT, HMS 'LION' AND 'IMPLACABLE' 1890 22467

The old ships of the line seen in photograph 22467, above, were probably used as training ships for young recruits. Outdated, mothballed or paid-off vessels were often moored at this spot off the mouth of Millbrook Lane. The much-loved aircraft carrier 'Ark Royal' spent some years here prior to being towed away for scrap in 1979. HMS 'Implacable', seen in this photograph, had one of the most extraordinary careers of any ship to sail. Launched in France in 1793 as the 'Duguay Trouin', at Trafalgar in 1805 she engaged Nelson's flagship, HMS 'Victory', and was eventually captured a few days later by HMS 'Hero'. Refitted at Devonport and renamed the 'Implacable', she fought in many battles before eventually becoming part of the HMS 'Lion' training establishment. She was decommissioned in 1904 and was eventually scuttled off the Isle of Wight in 1949.

In 1888 the Hoe became a park and the Armada Memorial (left of photograph 75908, below) was erected to mark the tercentenary of the great victory over the Spanish invasion fleet. The Naval Memorial was originally erected in 1920 to honour those killed in the First World War, and a sunken garden was added later to record the dead of the Second World War. A full alphabetical list of the 22,443 names on the memorial of the men and women who gave their lives is available from Plymouth Central Library and from the tourist information office. There are carved lions at the corners of the memorial and ship's prows at the pinnacle, which represent the four winds that blow: the angry north, the warm south, the bitter east and the kind west.

THE NAVAL AND ARMADA MEMORIALS 1924 75908

The attractive Halfpenny Bridge seen in this photograph is so named because of the charge of half a penny to cross it. Today, the whole area is unrecognisable: some of the creek has been filled in, the ramshackle huts have been demolished, and the banks are the home of leisure boat builders.

DEVONPORT, HALFPENNY BRIDGE 1904 52427

ONION SELLERS 1907 59208

Up North Hill, on the left just after Sherwell church, is Drake's Reservoir. The reservoir itself was built in 1849 on Drake's Leat, Plymouth's original water supply, which was built by Sir Francis Drake in 1590-91 at a cost of £300. The leat brought water seventeen miles from the head of the River Meavy, 'carried every way to get the vantage of the hills'. The distance as the crow flies is only nine miles, and the leat represents a fair engineering achievement. It not only supplied clean water to Plymouth, but also powered several mills. For the last 400 years, the bringing of fresh water to Plymouth by Drake has been celebrated by the annual 'Fyshinge Feaste' in June. The Mayor of Plymouth and his council congregate at the head weir of the leat, where official toasts are drunk, from a goblet filled with water from the leat, 'to the pious memory of Sir Francis Drake'. Another goblet, this time filled with red wine, is then passed round, with each person drinking a further toast: 'May the descendants of him who brought us water never want'. As part of the tradition, a meal of local trout caught from the leat is eaten.

Photograph 59208, opposite, shows two young lads, probably French, standing by the harbour wall with their strings of onions. With their grimy jackets and trousers, they give every impression of having endured an uncomfortable passage. For many years Plymouth, with its direct ferry service to Brittany, saw French onion sellers in the town every year.

The production of the first hard-paste, or 'true', porcelain was achieved in Britain by a chemist, William Cookworthy, in his Plymouth factory from 1768 to 1770. Known as 'Plymouth porcelain', it is distinguishable from the Bristol porcelain that he produced later by its imperfections. Examples can be seen in Plymouth City Museum and Art Gallery.

The Crownhill Fort, built in 1863, is known locally as Plymouth's best kept secret. This elaborate Victorian fort was the principal, and largest, fort of Plymouth's North-Eastern Defences, intended to defend the Royal Dockyard at Devonport from an attack by the French from the north. At the time of its construction Crownhill represented the cutting edge of fortress design and, because of its exposed position, was designed for all-round defence, making it unlike any other fort in the Plymouth defences. It has seven sides, each with massive ramparts, and is surrounded by a deep dry ditch; each flank of the fort was defended by gunfire from projecting caponiers. The anticipated threat from the French never materialised, and Crownhill and its guns were never put to the ultimate test. However, Crownhill was retained by the army for over a century and used by a succession of infantry regiments when the Fort was used as HQ Plymouth Garrison. It is believed that anti-aircraft guns were positioned inside the Fort during the Second World War, making it the only time that the Fort saw action. Its military use ended in 1983. In 1986 the Fort was sold to the Landmark Trust. It has now been restored and is open to visitors; the staff dress up in Victorian costumes, and offer period outfits for younger visitors, and there is a daily gun firing at 1.30pm, a reminder of Crownhill Fort's former role as part of Plymouth's mighty Victorian 'Ring of Fire'.

The Merchant's House in St Andrew's Street is a jettied, four-storey Jacobean house which was built in 1608 for William Parker. He was not only a privateer and a friend of Sir Francis Drake, but was also Lord Mayor of Plymouth in 1601-02. The house is now a fascinating museum which sheds light on many aspects of life in Plymouth in the past. There is a Victorian schoolroom, old fashioned chemist's shop, and an exploration of social inequality in the Rich Man's Room, but of particular interest is the information about the Plymouth Blitz and the rebuilding of the city, featuring the memories and experiences of local people.

THE DRAKE STATUE
1890 22364

CHARLES CHURCH 1889 22405

The building of Charles Street Church started in 1640 after Charles I gave permission for another parish to be created. Construction was suspended during the Civil War and completed in 1657. The church was dedicated to King Charles the Martyr in 1665. Once one of the finest post-Reformation Gothic churches in the country (see photograph 22405, above), Charles Church was gutted in the blitz of the Second World War; its ruins were retained as a memorial to Plymouth's war dead.

During the Second World War, thousands of people left Plymouth each night for the safety of the Dartmoor foothills to escape the bombs, returning to work in the city the next morning. The bombed shell of St Andrew's Church was planted with flowers so that people could continue to worship in the 'Garden Church', while on hot summer evenings crowds would come in their thousands from the ruined city to dance on the Hoe with dignitaries like Lady Nancy Astor, MP, and cock a defiant snook at Nazism.

The north side of Cobourg Street, seen in photograph P60038, below, is almost unchanged today. The Public Secondary School (right of photograph), whose most well-known old girl is the television personality Angela Rippon, is now part of the University of Plymouth, and the playground is occupied by satellite dishes.

COBOURG STREET c1940 P60038

THE PIER AND DRAKE'S ISLAND 1892 30583

Plymouth's pier (see above) was destroyed in the blitz. It was built in 1884, extending out from the old Bull Ring, a popular spot for political meetings, particularly in the 19th century during the noisy campaign that led in 1832 to Plymouth becoming three constituencies, and Devonport and Stonehouse having their own MPs for the first time. The centre of the pier was a popular venue for concert parties, boxing, wrestling, roller-skating and tea dances. To take the sea air in the company of other fashionable Victorians, one entered through the turnstiles on each side of the clock, for the princely sum of two pence.

In the 1920s and 1930s, transatlantic liners such as the 'Queen Mary' and the 'Normandie' anchored in the Sound. It was quicker to put in at Plymouth and transfer passengers to trains for London from Millbay Docks than it was to sail on to Southampton. Some famous passengers who travelled to London from Plymouth in this way were the film stars Charlie Chaplin, Mary Pickford and Rudolph Valentino.

Serving both a rural area round about, and hundreds of ports by way of trade, Plymouth reached its mercantile heyday in Victorian times. The railways arrived in 1848-49, and at last Plymouth had a rapid connection with the rest of the country, but for many years the Great Western Railway ended its journey at the city. Only with the construction of the Royal Albert Bridge across the Tamar to Saltash did the railway open up the Duchy of Cornwall. Isambard Kingdom Brunel's magnificent railway bridge across the Tamar, completed in 1859 shortly before his death, is a fitting memorial to the great Victorian engineer. The Admiralty stipulated that it must be at least 100ft above the water to allow the passage of ships beneath it.

SALTASH, THE ROYAL ALBERT BRIDGE 1890 22480

ST ANDREW'S CHURCH 1889 22399

Construction of St Andrew's Church began in 1370, and the tower was built by Thomas Yogge in 1481. The church was severely damaged by enemy bombing in 1941. Restoration of the church began in 1949, and it was reconsecrated in 1957, its modern altar and panes of stained glass (by John Piper) blending with the older fabric of the original building.

Drake's Island was originally known as St Nicholas Island. It was owned by the Priors of Plympton, who used it as a rabbit warren. It was fortified in 1549 and the defences were later extended by Sir Francis Drake - hence the name change. On his return from circumnavigating the world in 1580, Drake anchored in the lee of the island while he sent messengers ashore to check if Queen Elizabeth was still alive and, if so, whether he was still in favour. He managed to ensure the latter by sending several tons of Spanish gold to London.

In 1812 the famous Scots engineer John Rennie began the construction of the Breakwater (see photograph 31954, page 41). A massive undertaking which was not completed until 1841, the Breakwater was a crucial development. Generations of mariners such as Grenville, Howard and Raleigh had complained that the relatively narrow entrances to the Plym and Tamar were dangerous in foul weather; mariners would often run before the storm to anchor in the sheltered waters of Tor Bay. Now, all a gale-battered ship had to do was slip in through the eastern or western entrances and move into the lee of the Breakwater, with plenty of sea-room and calm water in which to anchor.

As a naval port, Plymouth has always had a large contingent of military personnel stationed around its various districts. Many impressive buildings, such as that seen in photograph 22448 (below) have been built to accommodate them.

DEVONPORT, ROYAL MARINE BARRACKS, STONEHOUSE 1890 22448

SALTASH, THE ROYAL ALBERT BRIDGE 1890 22477

The rich fields of the Tamar Valley have long been the source of Plymouth's fruit and vegetables. Tamar barges such as the one in the centre of photograph 22477 (above) would bring produce down from Calstock, Gunnislake and Bere Alston and land them at Cornwall Street in Devonport.

Secretary of the Navy Samuel Pepys, best known nowadays for his diaries but also effectively the founder of the Royal Navy as we know it, visited Plymouth with Charles II in 1676 to inspect sites for a new Royal Dockyard. Turnchapel, at the mouth of the Plym, was considered, but eventually the prize was given to the Tamar. The Tamar's disadvantages - strong tides, a narrow and winding entrance and often contrary winds - also acted in its favour as they gave the river natural defences from attack. Work started on what is now Devonport's South Yard in 1691.

In 1690 William III awarded a contract to build a stone dock on the Hamoaze to Robert Waters. The site chosen, in what is now South Yard, was excavated and a wet dock and a dry dock were built. The first ship built here, the 50-gun HMS 'Looe', was launched in 1696, and Dock, as it was then called, was established as a naval dockyard. It was extended to the north in 1719 with the building of the gun wharf (now Morice Yard). A series of wars over the next century, culminating in the Napoleonic Wars, ensured the expansion of the yard and the town that was growing up around it. It was not all plain sailing. Within a month of the end of the Napoleonic Wars, the navy had laid up 200 ships, 85% of the sailors had been discharged, and the dockyard was idle; there were over 7,000 paupers in Plymouth as a result. However, gradually the dockyard picked up again, helped by the increasingly pressing demands of running a far-flung empire. In 1844-54 the Keyham Steam Yard was built, and support services also developed in the area - the Victualling Yard at Stonehouse was built in 1824-35, Raglan Barracks in 1854-58, and the Royal Naval Engineering College was constructed near Keyham Yard in 1879-81. All these precious facilities required protection, and so the Sound was ringed with forts armed with the latest in gunnery: Drake's Island received granite casemates, Bovisand and Picklecombe were fortified, and further afield Tregantle and Cawsand forts were built. In all, by 1870 there were 29 forts defending the dockyard.

Sir Walter Raleigh is famous for introducing the ordinary potato to England from the New World, but Plymouth's Sir Francis Drake and Sir John Hawkins brought sweet potatoes to England in about 1563-65. Drake said of sweet potatoes: 'These potatoes be the most delicate rootes that may be eaten, and doe farre exceed our passeneps or carets. Their pines be of the bignes of two fists, the outside whereof is of the making of a pine-apple, but it is soft like the rinde of a cucomber, and the inside eateth like an apple but it is more delicious than any sweet apple sugared.' Sweet potatoes are now easily available in most supermarkets and greengrocer shops, and can be served in all the ways that ordinary potatoes are used, but cook much more quickly.

A monument in Freedom Park commemorates the 'Sabbath Day Fight' of the Civil War. The inscription reads: "Upon this spot on Sunday December 3rd 1643 after hard fighting for several hours the Roundhead Garrison of Plymouth made their final rally and routed the Cavalier Army which had surprised the Outworks and well nigh taken the town. For many years it was the custom to celebrate the anniversary long known as the 'Sabbath Day Fight' and recorded as the 'Great Deliverance' of the protracted siege successfully sustained by troops and Townsfolk on behalf of the Parliament against the King under great hardships for more than three years." Although Freedom Park is generally thought to take its name from the 'Sabbath Day Fight', another school of thought suggests that the name may go back as far as the 14th or 15th century. The annual Freedom Day Holiday commemorated the Breton raid of 1403, when a French fleet attacked and burnt Plymouth. Part of the celebrations was a mock battle between the Breton Boys and the Old Town Boys, an event which became so boisterous that it was eventually moved here, a safe distance from the town.

As well as being used for promenading, the Hoe has always been the vantage point from which Plymothians have watched the arrivals and departures of vessels. In the late 20th century the big events were the return of Sir Francis Chichester in 'Gypsy Moth IV', after his historic first single-handed voyage around the world in 1966-67, and later the return of battle-weary ships from the Falklands War. In the 21st century, the Hoe and all the hills around Plymouth were lined with thousands of people welcoming home Ellen MacArthur who, on February 7, 2005, broke the world record for the fastest solo circumnavigation of the globe.

The Plymouth-Dakar Challenge, first run in 2003 and since 2005 also known as the Plymouth-Banjul Challenge, is a car rally for charity. It very roughly follows the route of the more famous Dakar Rally, visiting many of the same countries. The challenge for the entrants is to drive an old banger worth approximately £100 from Plymouth to Africa, not in fact to Dakar, but further down the north-west coast of Africa to Banjul in Gambia, where the cars are auctioned for, or donated to, charity. The Challenge was the idea of Julian Nowell from Devon. It has now developed something of a cult following, and in 2005 the sum of £150,000 was raised for charities in the UK and Gambia.

THE BREAKWATER 1893 31954

OLD TOWN STREET 1889 22398

The oldest surviving domestic building in Plymouth is Prysten House, close to St Andrew's Church, in Finewell Street. It was built by Thomas Yogge in 1498, and is a fine limestone building with a galleried courtyard. The bottom floor of the house is let out as a restaurant, Tanners. In the past the building has been used as a dwelling house, a warehouse, a wine store and a bacon factory, but has belonged to St Andrew's Church since the 1920s and is used with the adjoining Abbey Hall for community purposes, and as a working museum. A model of Plymouth as it was in 1620 can be seen, and also of interest is the 28ft Plymouth Tapestry, which depicts the colonisation of America.

One of Devon's most famous sons was the former Royal Naval captain Robert Falcon Scott, 'Scott of the Antarctic.' He was born near Plymouth in 1868, and became a national hero when he set the new 'furthest south' record with his expedition to Antarctica on 'Discovery' in 1901-1904. He came within 410 miles of the South Pole on this expedition, and set out on a further attempt to be the first man to reach this point in 1910, on board the 'Terra Nova'. His team arrived in Antarctica on 11 January 1911, but ran into difficulties almost immediately when their mechanical sledges failed due to the cold, and their ponies had to be shot because they could not survive the weather. At the same time a second explorer, the Norwegian Amundsen, was also racing them to the South Pole; using dogs to pull his sledges, he made rapid progress and reached the Pole in December 1911. Scott's five-man team were unaware of this, and were running short of supplies. They reached the South Pole on 17 January 1912, only to find out the heartbreaking news that they had been beaten by the Norwegians. Their challenge now was to return safely to their base, but with the team suffering from starvation, hypothermia and other illnesses, this was not to be. Petty Officer Evans was the first to die, and then Captain Oates walked out of the party's tent on his 32nd birthday in March 1912, after delivering one of the most famous parting lines in history: 'I am just going outside and may be some time.' He never came back. As a blizzard raged outside the tent the other three team members could only await the inevitable, yet they were only 11 miles away from a fuel and food depot. Before his death, Scott wrote in his diary: 'We shall stick it out till the end, but we are getting weaker, of course, and the end cannot be far. It seems a pity but I do not think I can write more.'

UNION STREET 1889 22359

44

SPORTING PLYMOUTH

The 'Argyle' in the name of Plymouth Argyle Football Club is thought to derive from the name of a road, Argyll Terrace (sometimes known as Argyle Terrace). Two of the founders of the club, F Howard Grose and W Pethybridge, were living in the street at the time the club was set up. The name of the street is thought to be linked to the Argyll and Sutherland Highlanders, who were at times stationed in the town. The green in Argyle's shirt is also thought to be connected with the colours of the regiment, green and navy tartan.

Plymouth Albion Rugby Football Club has had at least five homes, including its present one at Brickfields Sports Facility. When the club moved to Bladderley in 1887, the admission price was three old pence - and players paid a penny to play!

Plymouth-born Sharron Davies is one of Britain's most successful swimmers. At the age of 13 she was the youngest member of the 1976 Olympic team in Montreal. She went on to win 20 British Championships, set 200 British records, and won a silver medal at the 1990 Olympic Games at Moscow, beaten to the gold medal by an East German who later admitted she was drug aided. In 1993, Sharron Davies was awarded the MBE. Since her retirement from competitive swimming she has helped to raise over £10 million for different charities, with her event 'Swim 4 Life'.

Plymouth is the home of the Azores and Back yacht race. The race was first contested in 1975, and takes place every four years. The course covers nearly 2,500 miles of ocean, and takes about 7-10 days in each direction.

Plymouth-born cricketer Laura Harper became the first female to be selected for a male regional team when she was chosen to play for the West of England under-15 team. She subsequently made her England debut at the age of 16 in 2000, and went on to play for her country in the 2000 World Cup in New Zealand.

QUIZ QUESTIONS

Answers on page 50.

1. Where will you find the Resurgam Door?

2. What was Plymouth's original name?

3. Which historic sea voyage began from Plymouth in 1577?

4. How did Prince Maurice Road and Mount Gould get their names?

5. What is the link between Plymouth and a notable 'first' in women's history?

6. Can you answer this old riddle?
   'Woman on a wheel,
   Ship on the sea,
   Eddystone Lighthouse,
   What can it be?'

7. Why in the past did women have to be careful which side of Union Street they walked down?

8. What was formerly known as the Crown and Anchor pub on the Barbican took its name from the arm insignia of naval Petty Officers - the name was often chosen for a pub by retired seamen who became landlords. The pub has undergone several name changes in the last 50 years - can you list them all?

9. What took four and a half years to complete, and is made up of 2,250,000 stitches, some of which were added by royalty - and where in Plymouth can you see it?

10. Which Plymouth-based artist is famous for her saucy paintings?

SMEATON'S TOWER AND THE BANDSTAND 1913 65979

RECIPE

'Great Drake, whose shippe aboute the world's wide wast
In three years did a golden girdle cast.
Who with fresh streames refresht this Towne that first
Though kist with waters, yet did pire for thirst.'

A dish of trout is traditional at the annual Fyshinge Feaste, which commemorates Sir Francis Drake bringing a supply of fresh water to Plymouth (see page 29).

TROUT WITH ALMONDS AND CREAM

Ingredients

4 trout, gutted and cleaned
Flour for coating the fish
Salt and pepper

175g/6oz butter
50g/2oz blanched almonds
Juice of half a lemon
150ml/¼ pint single cream

Mix the flour with salt and pepper and use to coat the fish on both sides. Melt 100g/4oz of the butter in a frying pan. Slide in the trout and cook for 15 minutes, turning halfway through cooking time, until they are golden brown on both sides and cooked through. Drain the trout and keep warm on a serving dish.

Clean the pan, then melt the remaining butter in it. Add the almonds and fry carefully until they are lightly browned. Stir in the lemon juice. Heat the cream gently in a separate pan and pour over the fish. Sprinkle with the almonds and serve.

RECIPE

DEVONSHIRE FLATS

Ingredients
225g/8oz self-raising flour
110g/4oz caster sugar
1 beaten egg

100ml/3½fl oz Devonshire
clotted or double cream
1 tablespoonful milk

Preheat the oven to 190 degrees C/375 degrees F/ Gas Mark 5.

Mix the flour and sugar together. Stir in the cream, egg and mix
thoroughly with enough milk to make a stiff dough. Roll out
the dough very thinly and cut into rounds of about 8cm/3 ins in
diameter. Sprinkle with a little sugar and bake for about ten minutes,
until lightly risen and golden brown.

QUIZ ANSWERS

1. While St Andrew's Church was still a smoking ruin after the blitz of Plymouth in 1941, someone wrote the word 'Resurgam' (Latin for 'I will rise again') above the door of the north porch. The church has now been rebuilt, and the door of the north porch has been known as the Resurgam Door ever since.

2. The use of 'Plymouth' as a name originates from the 13th century. Before then the settlement was called Sutton, a name that survives today for the harbour area.

3. Francis Drake began his historic circumnavigation of the world in the 'Golden Hind' from Plymouth in 1577; no other ship had ever made such a voyage before. When he returned to England in 1580 he was knighted by Elizabeth I. In 1966-67 Francis Chichester became the first man to sail single-handed around the world. He was knighted by Elizabeth II, using the same sword as that used by her predecessor for knighting Drake.

4. They are named after the Royalist and Parliamentarian commanders of the Civil War forces which fought at Plymouth in 1643, Prince Maurice and Colonel Gould.

5. Plymouth Sutton was represented in Parliament by Lady Nancy Astor from 1919-46, who was Britain's first woman MP. Lord and Lady Astor lived at 3 Eliot Terrace, next to the Grand Hotel on the Esplanade Hoe, and were also the much respected Mayor and Mayoress of Plymouth during the Second World War. Nancy Astor once complained to Winston Churchill: 'Winston, if you were my husband I would flavour your coffee with poison', to which Churchill replied: 'Madam, if I were your husband, I should drink it'.

6. An old-fashioned penny. All these symbols were on the obverse. The woman on a ship's wheel was Britannia, ruling the waves, with the Eddystone lighthouse to the left and a ship to the right. In 1859 the Royal Mint commissioned Leonard Charles Wyon to design new coinage with a new portrait of Queen Victoria, and the farthing, halfpenny and one penny coins featured the Eddystone Lighthouse to commemorate the centenary of its building by John Smeaton. A new design, showing the 1882 Eddystone lighthouse but without the ship to the right, was introduced in 1937 on one penny coins (see photograph F6050, opposite), and this remained on the penny until decimilisation in 1971.

7. Local lore has it that in earlier days respectable ladies stuck to one side of Union Street, and 'working girls' to the other, to avoid confusion!

8. In 1967 the Crown and Anchor was renamed the 'Sir Francis Chichester' to celebrate the achievements of the single-handed yachtsman; in 1989 it was renamed 'Pilgrims', to commemorate the departure of the Pilgrim Fathers to the New World in 1620; eight years later it became 'Bar PL1' after its postcode; and in 2002 it reverted to its original name. It has recently been revamped and again renamed, and is currently known as 'McShanes'.

9. The Plymouth Tapestry, which depicts the colonisation of America. It can be seen in Prysten House in Finewell Street.

10. Beryl Cook, who has lived in Plymouth for over 25 years. She originally came to the city to run a guesthouse, and began to paint in her late 40s. Her work is popular for its sense of fun and irreverence, full of ordinary, unassuming folk without pretensions but with a playful streak of vulgarity and naughtiness. Many of the flamboyant, fun-loving characters in her paintings were inspired by the lively pub life of Plymouth, and the Dolphin pub on the Barbican features in many of her works.

ONE PENNY PIECE, SHOWING THE EDDYSTONE LIGHTHOUSE 1948 F6050

UNION STREET 1904 52406

FRANCIS FRITH

PIONEER VICTORIAN PHOTOGRAPHER

Francis Frith, founder of the world-famous photographic archive, was a complex and multi-talented man. A devout Quaker and a highly successful Victorian businessman, he was philosophical by nature and pioneering in outlook. By 1855 he had already established a wholesale grocery business in Liverpool, and sold it for the astonishing sum of £200,000, which is the equivalent today of over £15,000,000. Now in his thirties, and captivated by the new science of photography, Frith set out on a series of pioneering journeys up the Nile and to the Near East.

INTRIGUE AND EXPLORATION

He was the first photographer to venture beyond the sixth cataract of the Nile. Africa was still the mysterious 'Dark Continent', and Stanley and Livingstone's historic meeting was a decade into the future. The conditions for picture taking confound belief. He laboured for hours in his wicker dark-room in the sweltering heat of the desert, while the volatile chemicals fizzed dangerously in their trays. Back in London he exhibited his photographs and was 'rapturously cheered' by members of the Royal Society. His reputation as a photographer was made overnight.

VENTURE OF A LIFE-TIME

By the 1870s the railways had threaded their way across the country, and Bank Holidays and half-day Saturdays had been made obligatory by Act of Parliament. All of a sudden the working man and his family were able to enjoy days out, take holidays, and see a little more of the world.

With typical business acumen, Francis Frith foresaw that these new tourists would enjoy having souvenirs to commemorate their days out. For the next thirty years he travelled the country by train and by pony and trap, producing fine photographs of seaside resorts and beauty spots that were keenly bought by millions of Victorians. These prints were painstakingly pasted into family albums and pored over during the dark nights of winter, rekindling precious memories of summer excursions. Frith's studio was soon supplying retail shops all over the country, and by 1890 F Frith & Co had become the greatest specialist photographic publishing company in the world, with over 2,000 sales outlets, and pioneered the picture postcard.

FRANCIS FRITH'S LEGACY

Francis Frith had died in 1898 at his villa in Cannes, his great project still growing. By 1970 the archive he created contained over a third of a million pictures showing 7,000 British towns and villages.

Frith's legacy to us today is of immense significance and value, for the magnificent archive of evocative photographs he created provides a unique record of change in the cities, towns and villages throughout Britain over a century and more. Frith and his fellow studio photographers revisited locations many times down the years to update their views, compiling for us an enthralling and colourful pageant of British life and character.

We are fortunate that Frith was dedicated to recording the minutiae of everyday life. For it is this sheer wealth of visual data, the painstaking chronicle of changes in dress, transport, street layouts, buildings, housing and landscape that captivates us so much today, offering us a powerful link with the past and with the lives of our ancestors.

Computers have now made it possible for Frith's many thousands of images to be accessed almost instantly. The archive offers every one of us an opportunity to examine the places where we and our families have lived and worked down the years. Its images, depicting our shared past, are now bringing pleasure and enlightenment to millions around the world a century and more after his death.

For further information visit: www.francisfrith.com

INTERIOR DECORATION

Frith's photographs can be seen framed and as giant wall murals in thousands of pubs, restaurants, hotels, banks, retail stores and other public buildings throughout Britain. These provide interesting and attractive décor, generating strong local interest and acting as a powerful reminder of gentler days in our increasingly busy and frenetic world.

FRITH PRODUCTS

All Frith photographs are available as prints and posters in a variety of different sizes and styles. In the UK we also offer a range of other gift and stationery products illustrated with Frith photographs, although many of these are not available for delivery outside the UK – see our web site for more information on the products available for delivery in your country.

THE INTERNET

Over 100,000 photographs of Britain can be viewed and purchased on the Frith web site. The web site also includes memories and reminiscences contributed by our customers, who have personal knowledge of localities and of the people and properties depicted in Frith photographs. If you wish to learn more about a specific town or village you may find these reminiscences fascinating to browse. Why not add your own comments if you think they would be of interest to others? See **www.francisfrith.com**

PLEASE HELP US BRING FRITH'S PHOTOGRAPHS TO LIFE

Our authors do their best to recount the history of the places they write about. They give insights into how particular towns and villages developed, they describe the architecture of streets and buildings, and they discuss the lives of famous people who lived there. But however knowledgeable our authors are, the story they tell is necessarily incomplete.

Frith's photographs are so much more than plain historical documents. They are living proofs of the flow of human life down the generations. They show real people at real moments in history; and each of those people is the son or daughter of someone, the brother or sister, aunt or uncle, grandfather or grandmother of someone else. All of them lived, worked and played in the streets depicted in Frith's photographs.

We would be grateful if you would give us your insights into the places shown in our photographs: the streets and buildings, the shops, businesses and industries. Post your memories of life in those streets on the Frith website: what it was like growing up there, who ran the local shop and what shopping was like years ago; if your workplace is shown tell us about your working day and what the building is used for now. Read other visitors' memories and reconnect with your shared local history and heritage. With your help more and more Frith photographs can be brought to life, and vital memories preserved for posterity, and for the benefit of historians in the future.

Wherever possible, we will try to include some of your comments in future editions of our books. Moreover, if you spot errors in dates, titles or other facts, please let us know, because our archive records are not always completely accurate—they rely on 140 years of human endeavour and hand-compiled records. You can email us using the contact form on the website.

Thank you!

For further information, trade, or author enquiries
please contact us at the address below:

**The Francis Frith Collection, Frith's Barn, Teffont,
Salisbury, Wiltshire, England SP3 5QP.**
Tel: +44 (0)1722 716 376 Fax: +44 (0)1722 716 881
e-mail: sales@francisfrith.co.uk **www.francisfrith.com**